Penny Pepper is a writer, poet a
life as a published poet began i
evolved into songwriting and flo
disability arts scene. This is her fi

An accomplished spoken word artist, her one woman show, Lost in Spaces, premiered at the Soho Theatre, London before going on a national tour. She has also performed widely including Trafalgar Square, The Olympic Park, Edinburgh Fringe Festival and New York.

She writes regularly for The Guardian and has appeared on Newsnight, BBC Radio 5 Live, Radio 4's Today programme and was featured on Woman's Hour, for their 70th birthday edition. She is named in the Power 100 of Britain's most influential disabled people.

Her explicit taboo-breaking book about sex and disabled people *Desires Reborn*, was published in 2012, and in 2013 she won a Creative Future Literary Award. Her memoir, *First In The World Somewhere*, is published by Unbound.

Penny is finishing work on her novel, *Fancy Nancy*. She likes cats, is a music junkie and once won an Erotic Oscar.

Website: http://www.pennypepper.co.uk

Twitter: @penpep

Come Home Alive

Penny Pepper

Burning Eye

Burning Eye Books
Never Knowingly
Mainstream

This edition published by Burning Eye Books 2018

www.burningeye.co.uk

@burningeyebooks

Burning Eye Books
15 West Hill, Portishead, BS20 6LG

ISBN 978-1-911570-48-6

Printed & bound by ImprintDigital.com, UK

Come Home Alive

CONTENTS

LOST IN SPACES

Bleary excitement on the children's ward;
I'm almost nine and counting up the stars,
Sharp-bright, distant and unexplored –
Are there rings round Saturn, and red dust on Mars?

On telly the stay-up treat is men in space.
I gaze at the flicker, misty black and white.
The NASA men speak in a hiss, a haste.
We're up from the bed; I'm going to take flight.

I want to float off into weightless skies;
This is Major Pen to Ground Control.
Look back at Planet Earth through different eyes,
Be mistress of the moon that I patrol.

But broken kids don't star in big space shows.
You never see us scorch across your screen.
We do not compute – as every robot knows.
Danger, Will Robinson! Life is not a TV scene.

Yet I yearn for the great beyond;
Commencing countdown, engines – go.
To boldly reach where no cripple girl has gone!
Horizon's wide, I won't look back below.

I'm rolling through the once-sealed door
And floating in a most unexpected way.
Planet Pen evolves, a universe to explore,
And yes. There's everything to say.

BOOKWORM

Peter and Jane go up the hill.
But I want to go through the wardrobe
Where Narnia lies on the other side.
I want to be in the Famous Five,
To chase the spies and be a tomboy.
I want the world I find in books.

The naughtiest girls at the poshest schools,
Tucking in to midnight feasts.
Jolly japes and playing pranks.
Are you in the Anglo-Saxon league?
Houses at school for Grace and Daphne.
This is the world I find in books.

Ballerinas at the barre,
Arabesques danced en pointe,
The tutu puffs in perfect pink.
Accidents and cripple teachers
But always the girl who becomes a star.
This is the world I find in books.

Up the mountains with smiley Heidi.
Granddad is scary and I don't like Peter.
Switzerland, it's clean and pure.
I wonder, if I could breathe the air,
Would I walk like Clara if I'm good?
This is the world I find in books.

Mary scowls and spoilt Colin whines –
A secret garden, the boy with robins
Makes us happy, he's kind and bold.
Colin walks tall when he tries hard.
Positive thinking will cure us all.
This is the world I find in books.

I take a pen and write some words
To tell the stories I never found.

Of poor kids, crip kids, kicking out.
Where girls fly free and save the world.
Adventures made for everyone.
This is the world I'll make in books.

LINDA

I learned the truth behind the screen
On the ward, aged fourteen,
From Linda, who was seventeen.
She was the greatest girl I'd seen
In bomber jacket white and green,

On her thin legs the skinny jeans,
Linda in her velveteens.
On Linda, who was seventeen,
Wrist-splints sparkled with a gleam,
Sovereign of her fashion scene.

Fornication on the TV screen.
I asked her, what did it mean?
Linda, who was seventeen,
She laughed until the credits streamed,
She taught me stuff they called obscene.

She had a boyfriend; he was keen,
Linda's sexy teenage dream.
Linda, who was seventeen,
She sucked bananas like a queen,
Dirty, dangerous and unclean.

She gave me hope, belief, esteem,
Subverted all their old regimes,
Linda, who was seventeen,
When adolescence made me scream
On that cusp and in between.

MEETING THE STRANGER

Chilly shower, hard cobbled path.
Handsome stranger, night-time hair.
Wishful murmurs, husky laugh,
Kneeling close beside my chair.

How, I wonder, do I seem?
Labels loud yet labels blurred.
I take him in, and hold a dream,
Musing as to if he's stirred.

The gulf between us might be there.
Symbols still define my form.
Yet in his eyes I sense fresh air
Dismissing fear out from a storm.

The ache is small and, newly felt,
It burns. I want to know this man.
Yet lines are drawn by what life dealt.
Seduction knows no certain plan.

Am I assumed a sexless wretch?
Or is my fear false skin I've grown?
I want your gaze to be a letch.
You'll kiss me as your wanton own.

MAMMOGRAM

My spongy flesh is clamped on the cold slab
while outside there's birds, there's flowers and leaves.
As these harsh blank sisters tut and murmur
I'm nothing but meat on a medical rack
suddenly, only a trussed and twisted breast
trying to think of the fragile autumn sun.

But they loom and blot out the fading sun
because I'm difficult on the dull grey slab
as it rises and bleeps upon my breasts.
The young nurse is kinder, tries hard, yet leaves
me to the witch, spinning her dark bladderwrack
that binds my grit, ties up my baby murmurs.

Inside out, naked, I barely murmur,
losing who I am, denied the sun,
turned a specimen on the demanding rack.
I'm flattened, a baker's leftover slab
of pasty dough that everyone leaves.
Who will love such pale tormented breasts?

Mum's body argued darkly once and her breast
was off as doctors reduced her to murmurs
of scalpels and skin veined like old maple leaves
though she thrived, her smile like a rising sun
full of *oh well* and laughter as she ate a slab
of chocolate, kept on my nan's old kitchen rack.

My mammaries stretch on their medics' rack.
I grasp thoughts of love – hands warm on my breasts
that first time by the grey-brown rocky slabs
of coastal stones, you coaxed my murmurs,
as we slipped ourselves through the sea and sun.
Kisses down my neck, you sigh once and leave.

The machine jolts and whines, as I glimpse leaves
through the dusty window, retreat from their rack.
The nurse shifts around, scowling back the sun,
as my eyes burn and pain riddles my breast.
I'm a wretched storm, see starlings in their dark murmurs.
At last a click. I pull back from the slab.

I rush to hide my murmurs and my breasts.
Autumn stays soft but the sun breaks the rack.
I'm wistful for leaves, your kiss – chocolate, big slabs.

DIDGERIDOO

The man with the boldest didgeridoo
came striding in from far away.
My flesh went flip, my fuses blew.

I'm freshly thralled in quite a stew
for him who's hard and dark in play —
the man with the biggest didgeridoo.

He grabbed me and my morals flew.
Thoughts go high, lust goes wahey.
My flesh went flip, my fuses blew.

Ashamed to say then love stuff grew
while he turned cold to colours grey,
the man with the darkest didgeridoo.

I spread my treasures wide and true.
He moulded me an easy prey.
My flesh went flip, my fuses blew.

He gulped me whole and had a chew,
now owning up and love turns blue
for the man with the broken didgeridoo,
my flesh still flip, all fuses glue.

MASHED UP

My first kitchen; a boiling pot,
food we want and always hot.
With vast potatoes a jiggling fury
to the cockney capers of Ian Dury.

Tomorrow is sex and drink and fun.
There will be more unpeelings done
in hungry corners, smeared wide-lipped.
I'm anxious, and I'm always chipped,
all wet soft-eyed blubber and squeak
when Alan's hand runs on my cheek,
mutters *love ya* at shaking skin,
and then the luscious melt begins.

Still, those potatoes stay hard blocks
and we're gloomy starving as we rock.
Alan pulls my skirt's elastic,
tells me I'm so crip fantastic.
But we've the cruel grey no-spud blues
and we both know only that which glues –
pleasure from the buttered mash
that slides and slips, a salty brash
murmuration of earthy ooze
down avid rebel throats with booze.

Aeons moved, light rose, light fell.
It came to pass – a mountain swell.
I pulped the spud, a luscious mound,
with the ancient fork I found.

We both know there's more to slake.
We're lust-roasted to a perfect bake.
And laugh as we lick, for fast dessert,
the mashed-up spud on my ripped tartan skirt.

A SPOKEN WORD LOVE POEM

Candlelight and stars
making patterns
quiver on the sea
in a restaurant
by Hastings Pier.

I toy with my mackerel,
full of thoughts
of when it swam
in its
happy swimmy sea.

My lover's blue eyes catch mine,
misty hazel from Merlot.
He lifts my hand
across the frosty linen tablecloth
and says, I wrote you a poem.

I blush
above my fish floating on the briny white plate

Tell me now, I sigh,
what poetry lurks
in that head
behind those glinting eyes,
what words will come
from the upturn
of your sweet mouth?

I still my breath.
The stars pause in their
tiny brilliance.

The world waits.

Tits! he says.
I love your tits!

Your bestest bits
Is your tits.
Fit tits, pert tits.
Tits to rate.
Your tits are fucking great!

I spear the cold mackerel
through its belly,
heart chilled and shaking,
and wonder at the world.

MY LOVE FOR YOU

My love for you is reckless and insane,
But my seething brain seeks no remedy;
For you and me love is a double game.

Rules and reasons are too dull and plain
And you're a changing drama like the sea.
My love for you is reckless and insane.

Loving you is pleasure mixed with pain.
You flow and fly and suddenly I'm free –
For you and me love is a double game.

I feel your velvet love inside my veins,
The curse of lust, its hold, its ecstasy –
My love for you is reckless and insane.

In you there's strength, a force I cannot tame,
But at your core red vulnerability;
For you and me love is a double game.

You love me inside out and back again
Till I can't tell the truth: who's you, who's me.
My love for you is reckless and insane;
For you and me love is a double game.

SUNFLOWERS

You make me believe yellow
is more than the clichéd sun,
a panoply of explosive nuance.
The stroke on each petal
a twist to the yolk –
through spectrums of possibility.
Darker ochre
and spark of lemon.
I ache to stroke the rays,
maybe lick the mustard.
Feel what you felt,
dance my fingers into the crevices,
banana curves and velvet slicks,
breathing, showy things.

THE LOVER

for L

All the while I give my love and shelter
He strays as if he has no place to go.
Always there some warning and some fracture.
He braces, fearing war and dreading snow.

Dealing only cards that doom his future,
He travels like he'll never stay again,
Gambling gifts of concrete and my nurture,
Pulls apart my heart he knows he's slain.

Explores within my welcome open nature.
He grasps my certain flesh, some dying thane.
Burning up the summer's light and splendour,
Fierce in his fight, he jousts against the grain.

I peel his layers quickly in my rapture,
The blood we spill burns through our favourite game.
We bite and claw in long and hot adventure;
When we flew together, how we came.

Despair and fury roiling at his centre,
Damage in the dark and from life's blame.
Yet where he goes he knows I cannot venture,
So he crushes love to morsels and a stain.

He wanders on beneath a moon in winter.
His conscious ploys will find him warmth and gain.
A posing knight, he grins with sorry censure.
My poor heart shakes – he'll have my gifts again.

A PRE-RAPHAELITE BLIZZARD

I went to you in the blizzard.
Snow fell in a frosting of tears.
Your heart that was beaten and withered
Awoke from a sleep of great years.

You're still that pale man who shivered,
Whose words are icicled spears.
They hang like lost dogs on a gibbet –
Howling, but no one shall hear.

I ache to the thoughts that I savour,
Like Janey in her lost lonely years,
And at your dark door how I waver –
Wondering who will appear.

You smile and here is my refuge,
The moonlight shines a way near.
My pellucid skin blushes red rouge
As you kiss me away from my bier.

But we know when love should be shattered.
We know what is wrong is unclear.
For a moment, a pause, we mattered,
And that memory is worth any fear.

SPECIAL

Fucking special

Special needs
Special time
Special breeds

Special case
Special care
Special race

Special knife
Special spoon
Special life

Special drink
Special food
Special stink

Special school
Special bus
Special rule

Fucking special

Special kids
Special thumb
Special flids

Special beds
Special charts
Special meds

Special arm
Special leg
Special charm

Special nurse
Special home
Special curse

Special job
Special step
Special nob

Fucking special

Special play
Special work
Special pay

Special shark
Special loan
Special mark

Special dosh
Special laws
Special cosh

Special ops
Special pain
Special cops

Special crip
Special time
Special chip

Fucking special

Special punk
Special hair
Special spunk

Special specs
Special sight
Special sex

Special dress
Special girls
Special mess

Special gun
Special boys
Special one

Special friend
Special death
Special end

I AM FUCKING SPECIAL.

SIX JOBS OSBORNE

Six Jobs Osborne, first name George,
Was said to strive and push and forge
For Uber lucre more, more – more!
Despite dosh, Gideon's a *Standard* bore.

BUS

On the bus,
Boris bus,
dirty bumpy
horrid bus.

There's a trolley in the crip space –
see the child, snotty-faced –
bullish buggy, hellish mummy,
disposition far from sunny.

On the bus,
double decker,
smelly shaky
bony wrecker.

There's a suitcase in the crip space,
nervous girl who grips in haste,
snarling hoodie chomping burger.
Doesn't he know that meat is murder?

On the bus,
Boris bus,
dirty bumpy
horrid bus.

Another journey, ramp is broken,
access just an empty token?
Public selfish, my dismay,
while driver grunts and looks away.

On the bus,
double decker,
smelly bumpy
bony wrecker.

In my slot a man with doggy –
by my shoulder youth who's groggy,

armpits foul, hair is stinking,
smells of vomit and binge drinking.

On the bus,
Boris bus,
dirty bumpy
horrid bus.

There we were such humble cripples,
fought the system, sent out ripples –
now to take a London bus
with the throng to push, to fuss –

On the bus,
Boris bus,
dirty bumpy
Tory bus,
any bus,
big or small,
dirty, rough,
crowded, empty,
loud and surly…

Scarcely
just a London
bus.
Not
much
fucking
use to us.

HANDBAGGED

What have you got in your handbag, dear?
What have you got in there?
Dad in the photo proud
Outside that Grantham shop?
What have you got in there?

Dennis's gold fountain pen,
His thick and open chequebook?

Shiny old milk bottle tops
From the drinks you snatched from kids?

Ronnie Raygun's sheriff badge,
The pistol locked and loaded?

A lock of Cecil's lovely hair,
His shameful resignation note?

Rude Heseltine and helicopter,
Echoes of his Tarzan yodel?

Scattered brains from the *Belgrano*,
The many seas of mothers' tears?

What have you got in your handbag, dear?
What have you got in there?
Arthur Scargill's wrinkled balls
Pinned inside a velvet box?
What have you got in there?

News clippings of the Greenham camps,
Eccentric women, dressed like tramps?

Tony Blair's sweet thank-you notes?
If not for you, Tone waned on votes.

From silent mother what did you take?
The little prayer book by mistake?

Your lady's muff somehow all lost,
Thrown away to a personal frost?

What have you got in your handbag, dear?
What have you got in there?
Your stubborn heart you kept on ice,
Thawed for when you must be nice?
What have you got in there?

FRAUD

You poke and prod my pocket
As servants clear your moat,
While I'm wheeling and I'm walking
In a ragged shabby coat.

You snatch and crush our wages
As servants shine your Rolls,
While we're shouting and we're swaying
In sparse seventh-hand clothes.

You cling to your policies
Like a brat with a dummy,
While we dig in poor-paid gutters
For a glimmer of some honey.

Granddad struggles in the morning,
Whimpers gently towards the night,
Sitting in his own hot shit
'Cause his care scheme's not paid right.

What kind of warped-out world
Is this one I see unfolding?
Our rulers fudging porno, second homes
And any chi-chi smallholding.

Independent Living Fund
Once helped us live full lives.
You killed our basic freedoms
And so many rights deprived.

Hypocrisy, it is on trend
And avarice shouts loud.
Bankers' greed bloats rulers' schemes.
Tax dodgers smirking proud.

We're scratching and we're whining
For free morsels and a crumb.

Recession, we're heaped with the blame
While those bastards hold the guilty gun.

Together we can win this fight
Against the rulers' gluts,
Fat with their ideology;
Act now – and fuck the cuts!

AFTERTHOUGHT

I am the afterthought
the special needs
embarrassment
on wheels or stick
the dribble and the stain
spastic you don't want to meet

I am the nuisance
the blind cunt idiot
you don't want to deal with

the stutter and the stumble
a deaf fuck annoyance
you have no time for

the ranting and the waving
loopy mental shit
in that street
you cross to avoid

the smelly old bitch
pooing her pants
staggering on the pavement
who you want to push over

alien on my planet
foreigner in all my lands
hated immigrant at my own home

I am the remnant
you want to forget
the history omission
not quite yet revised

Yet.
I am me
and I am your neighbour

your sister and brother
your offspring born and imminent
your parent, your lover, your friend
I am omnipresent
and, believe me, I am you
and I am yours

SCROUNGER

I'm a sponger, a scrounger,
A lazy-arsed lounger,
A raspberry in rainbow.
I pose you no danger.
I'm the bottomless pit
Of your pity and debt,
On the sick since John Major;
I'm still on it yet!

I'm the latest cheap target,
Tabloids' dark darling
Draining the markets –
The unit of measure
Economic displeasure.

I'm a blamed useless eater,
A foul fraud repeater.
Do I make it all up?
They say that I suck
The money from purses
Of rich bloated bastards.
The kicks and the curses
Fall from our leaders
On us liars and bleeders.
We're pariahs and feeders,
Gorged on too much
From the big nanny state.
You've condemned us already.
There is no debate.

We can't be sustained
Because bankers are greedy.
We're lazy, we're rank,
We're targets of hate
To e-rad-icate!

But I'm a rouser with words

To shout and to hit,
Saying who are the Nazis
Raking over this shit?

I shout and I spin
At the string of their lies.
I'm a new Boadicea.
Together we rise!

They have no compassion.
Yet we own rebellion,
and rage with our passion.
As time it is rushing,
defiance it chimes!

We dare to fight back.
We dare to fight loud.

WE
DARE
WE
DARE
WE
DARE

JESUS SAVED ME IN PEACOCKS

Jesus saved me in Peacocks
By the purple stiletto heels.
Well, a woman told me he loves me,
That he understands how I feel.

Maybe it's true that in Peacocks
Many gods lurk in the clothes,
The rumpled slave-laboured undies,
The dresses in disordered rows.

I flew down the aisles in Peacocks
Searching for Krishna and Zeus.
I paused by the thongs for reflection
But Jehovah was not hanging loose.

There's plenty of healing in Peacocks
Of the retail therapy kind.
Cheapies for chavvies and cripples.
We know that Jesus don't mind.

I've not had more signs when I'm shopping
That I'm cured from my devilish ways,

So I'll live my life with some relish,
Be a peacock in outrageous display.

ON MILLENNIUM BRIDGE

Rain slips through springy steel,
Tyres squeal in the grooves,
My wheelchair a juicy nuisance.

Brief smiles replace the scowls,
Cameras click, memories freeze.
I ignore the crowds and drizzle,

Pass over the river's grey divide,
Caught between gallery and cathedral,
An uncertain leper-pilgrim

Crossing decrepit Londinium.

CRIPPLEGATE TOWN

Give me ten pork chops, twelve gallons of ale.
Plague will chase us to our death; leap close to hear my tale.
We don't look like the king and queen of this or any land,
But we're staying and we're shouting, sat firm to take a stand.

There's deaf, there's blind, there's wailers, the war-hacked with
    their sticks.
We gather at old Cripplegate for a morsel by its bricks.
Bold Alice had the pox last year; her face can still make trade,
Though highborn ladies with nosegays make sport and trot away.

Edward entertains the lords and throws a splendid hobble,
He rolls and shakes those stumps around and turns a dandy
    wobble.
It's years away to Bedlam days, perchance we'll blame the devil –
Rip my clothes, I am possessed, my hair's alarmed, dishevelled.

Harold rings a begging bell, his leper's nose unseen,
But underneath his wretched shirt, Alice knows what's keen!
By the wall of our saint's church, it's all about St Giles –
Yet if we see a pious man, we lose our godly smiles.

Shiny farthings shower fast upon the crippled throng.
Make sure the priests don't scoop them first; each sings a greedy
    song.
How can the law say invalids can't wave our begging plate?
This is the life we're forced to live, so we haunt this Cripplegate.

Come to Cripplegate, come to Cripplegate, come to Cripplegate
    town.

You see me sway in my fine clothes, proud upon my frame –
I throw their insults to the wind and other words reclaim.
Like ancient cripples by that gate, I'll make my mark, be sure.
I am here and if you're good, I'll lead you through my door…

Tempus fugit, time it flies, yet much goes on the same –

Disabled people's open bowls rust with a different name.
Young soldiers lurch to hearth and home, minus limbs and eyes,
Bright heroes for a summer's day, then fraudsters to despise.

Pull up your socks, you slacking plebs, government now utters.
The mental, and the chronic ill, discarded down the gutters.
Some crippled folk get sporty, win Paralympic gold,
But if you don't bring money in, they wish you dead and cold.

Once again, the circle's turned, fresh wastrels you can hate.
We're scroungers and we're spongers for the tabloids to berate.
But let us say we're born of you and likely you will see
No one cuts the perfect cloth; rebuke that fallacy.

A lifestyle choice? It's never one; wake up and see the fact.
Beware the oily rhetoric of our leaders' foul attack.
Humanity is broad and wide, its patterns vast and great.
We are no bland homogeny – accept and celebrate.

Come to Cripplegate, come to Cripplegate, to my Cripplegate
    town.

DISABILITY IS

Steps into the pub
No way to get up

Steps up to the bog
No lights in the shop

Hand rail snaps
Busting a crap

No BSL known
Cold to each bone

No lights to get home
No access to phone

Bus ramp broken
Insults spoken

No carer at night
No help in sight

All fake disabled
Harsh laws tabled

Not worth a wage
Despise our rage

Not worth a look
Small-printed book

Uncaring of lack
More money cutbacks

Means slashing wrists
Government shits

Phlegm-sopping shouts
From privileged louts

Money they block
Keeps us crock

Disability is
What you chop
What you take
What you stop
What you never
create.

COME HOME ALIVE

If you come home alive, my lad,
We'll tell you it's best you'd died.
My lad, my lad, my loveliest lad,
Really much better you died.

We liked you best with legs, my lad,
With arms, my lad, a face, my lad.
My lad, my lad, my loveliest lad,
Really much better you'd died.

We'd like you laid in a grave, my lad.
You'll make a hero dead, my lad.
My lad, my lad, my loveliest lad,
Really much better you died.

A victor, a coward, who cares, my lad?
Doesn't look good if you live, my lad.
My lad, my lad, my loveliest lad.
Less fuss. Less cost if you're dead.

TOP OF HIS POPS

Top of his pops, straight in at number ten!
Nine, Jimmy Savile's on kiddie ward again.
Eight o'clock bell, nearly time for bed,
Seven, still awake in dread.
Six times four, no one knows –
Five kids curl up toes.
Four comes the hand –
Three, demand
Two, I'm
One.

CHURCH IN THE WOOD

A vast hot
Hand
Takes mine.
Coaxes me
To the church in the wood.

I smell the bonfires
As we walk through
Naked trees,
Their branches bent in
To the church in the wood.

He smells of sweat and candles
In his funny black dress.
Eyes look down as
He pulls at his white collar
In the church in the wood.

A velvet curtain comes around,
Around, around me.
Our Father which art in heaven.
Hands, breath, fingers – pain
In the church in the wood.

His whispers and hisses.
Pray for forgiveness
Or you shall be punished.
Deliver us from evil.
In the church in the wood.

LETTER TO THE GREY MAN IN 1974

Dear man with the grey hair
standing there in the dark,
with your camera.
I was ten.
Did I need to take
my clothes right off?

Dear man with the grey hair –
yeah, you were a doctor
in a stupid white coat.
When you were ten
in 1974
you did as you was told.

Dear man with the grey hair,
I hated that big chart
you stretched me on.
At ten, quiet,
shaking and blushing,
my painful arm pulled.

Dear man with the grey hair,
breathing hard on my cheek,
twisting me back –
small for ten,
you said, your smile wrong,
your fingers too close.

Dear man, I know you're dead now.
Took your curse to my guts,
a poison that spread far
beyond ten.
It travelled – heart and thought,
attracted a black dog.

Dear man who is bad bones,
I spewed you out hard.
Shred your grey hair
ten times ten.
At last, I burnt the chart.

BORDERLINE TOWN

There's a fist and a kiss in Borderline town.
My heart hears the calling and soon I must go
Into battle clutching my blood-drenched gown.

The voices sing sweet and tempt me to drown
In sorrow that's slick, singing words that I know.
There's a fist and a kiss in Borderline town.

I hold my guard but I'm dragged right down,
Strangled on spirals of thoughts I don't own,
Into battle clutching my blood-drenched gown.

The cuts and the questions, not quickly found,
With tears a fountain that beats on each bone.
There's a fist and a kiss in Borderline town.

A thousand raw needs deny me renown
As overload turns my tongue to stone,
Into battle clutching my blood-drenched gown.

The past a giant in a devilish crown
Where children get crushed into deep unknowns.
There's a kiss and a fist in Borderline town.
Into battle, surrender my blood-drenched gown.

YOU DON'T UNDERSTAND

You don't understand
The class-ridden side of it
The hidden deride of it
You don't understand

You don't understand
The denigration and hurt
The indignant cold blurt
You don't understand

You don't understand
Obvious, you see
Hate to be useless me
You don't understand

You don't understand
Explain this foul view
I'm inferior to you?
You don't understand

You don't understand
When unrest shouts back
We expose what you lack
You will understand

BLING

Please let me bling my invalid tray.
It's dull and it's worthy,
Might as well be grey.
I love it 'cause I need it
And it helps me work and play,
But oh, Lord, let me bling my invalid tray.

I got a bit of plastic.
Does it make me feel fantastic?
Does it label me – spastic?
It makes me feel sarcastic
But I'm iconoclastic.

Let me bling this thing,
Make my lickle world sing.
I'm rhyming, I'm dining,
It's Perspexing.
Let me do it.
Let me screw it.
Let me free with da bling.

Enthusiastic,
I'm full fashionastic.
Purple-green I dash it.
With colour I will splash it.
Make me orgiastic.

Let me bling this thing,
Make my lickle world sing.
I'm rhyming, I'm dining,
It's Perspexing.
Let me do it.
Let me skew it.
Let me free with da bling.

Let me free,
Let me free,
Let me free
With da bling.

EVIDENTLY LEYTONSTONE (1984)

after John Cooper Clarke

The bloody dogs they bloody shit,
Make the pavement bloody foul.
A bloody granny, bloody hit
By bloody skinheads on the prowl.
I'm bloody stuck, I'll bloody moan.
Evidently Leytonstone.

Bloody Thatcher bloody hates
Bloody miners' bloody strikes.
Hang bloody Scargill on gates,
Slap the bloody Greenham dykes.
I'm bloody fucked, I'll bloody moan.
Evidently Leytonstone.

Bloody buses, bloody steps,
On the bloody sick again.
Bloody pills to bloody depths,
Bloody wheelchair, bloody pain.
It's bloody crap when no one's home.
Evidently Leytonstone.

Social worker's bloody crap,
Bloody nothing bloody done.
Bloody carer, bloody naps,
Bloody stuck, no bloody fun.
No bloody sex, no bloody groans.
Evidently Leytonstone.

I bloody dream of going forth
With bloody girls and bloody mouths.
Bloody twats from bloody north,
Poor bleed too in bloody south.
London bleeds in ghetto zones.
Evidently Leytonstone.

ENGLAND EXPECTS

By Nelson's big tomb Mum stood briefly.
We hadn't expected it there in the crypt
Of giant St Paul's with its famous dead,
Under the mighty implausible dome.
Mum was concerned with Ivor Novello,
His plaque on a shadowy wall.
He was a famous singer, she said brightly,
In case I didn't know.

HYMN TO DADDY

Sixties magic-hour made
Golden glow in summer shade.
Special school bus brings me back
To my suburban cul-de-sac.
Daddy, Daddy, I twist to find
The photographs that haunt my mind,
And break your spell, before dusk falls
To make dark shadows down the hall.

Dashing hero and blackest hair,
I see you standing, smiling there
As the light begins to fade,
And dims the flowers to softly greyed,
I'm in the garden in my blue skirt
Where you kissed away my hurt.
Then you left before dusk falls
To make dark shadows down the hall.

Put away your photos now.
That's as much as I'll allow.
My daddy, you will not come back.
All your colours fade to, black.
Shut the album, close the book.
I can't take another look.
Daddy's gone, and now dusk falls.
There are no shadows. There is no hall.

BEAD EYE

It's an apolog-
Eye.
A dot.
Optical.
Twitches.
Your reptilian past.

Ringed
White spectacles
For the bead.
Dark as glass
In a forgotten church.

Your neck
Elongates
At motion
The bead detects.
Then the bobbing
As you walk on.
Birds around you
On stumps, minus
Bits and pieces,
As your magnet
Draws you to food.

Yet I cry
When the bead
Is closed, or made
An obscure smear
Into the mess of you
On a road.

FOSSIL HUNTING

We were bold and brave that windy dawn
By the dim and dancing sea of Dorset,
Its sand and shells and stones all singing.
Bone and blood and bivalves stray here
And ghosts of great gone beasts gather
By our hands, harassing slate in hearts.

CATS WHISKERS

a poem into song

Delightfully excusable is what you'll always be,
So, refusing nothing in my melancholy,
You'll do for something,
You'll do very well
For me.

Tie me to the tracks and the train can run me down.
I need you, please believe it,
So don't let's fall
To a sad life-lashing frown.

Even as I hold myself,
Afraid now of the dark,
Clouds of shadowed misery
Might tease
But soon depart,
For you are held inside my thoughts and fears
And turn to warmth these small cold hands
That catch all anxious tears.

Curl up and clutch tranquillity.
You call me so romantically.
Tug the thread that binds us
Through heart and flesh and head.
These lonely days might bind us
But miss the grave
And find a tender bed.
Oh, everything in whispers.
Let love hold high our heart.
Oh, the real cat's whiskers,
That's what you are...

'Cats Whiskers' is on the eponymous LP Spiral Sky, *1992,
Acme Records.*

A SONG TO HASTINGS

With its pebbles and its sinking beach,
A sea that tempts to never reach
The pretty painted houses high,
As white sky-bound the seabirds circle
The people hugged around the shore.
This is Hastings seaside town,
Cheery, coastal Hastings.

With cat creeps and twittens sly
As that word from older times.
This is Hastings with steep inclines
And tiny windy alley sneaks, says a no
To me in my wheelchair mode.
This is Hastings seaside town,
A teasing, haunted Hastings.

The seagulls mewl and poo-poo-poo,
Grabbing ice creams, bags of chips.
Birds bomb Hastings, nips on wings
Loving thermals by the sea.
Guerrilla bird, you're bold to me.
This is Hastings seaside town,
Bright, bawdy, boozy Hastings.

Bumpy path on Rock-a-Nore
To take me near the swelling sea,
An outpost of the windswept cliffs,
Of jagged sand-hued geology.
Birds lift on air, as dark waves flare
Against the pebbles' constant hiss,
Rattle-shells twist in the brine.
This is Hastings seaside town.
My heart is yours, old Hastings.

BONFIRE

They're coming, they're coming, the drummers are a-coming.
I hear them, I hear them, on the sea front drumming.

The crowding, it's crowding, the people fill the roads.
I see them, I see them, the young, the tall, the old.

The thronging, the thronging procession comes a-singing.
I hear them, I hear them, with sticks and bells a-ringing.

The torches, the torches, the fire and smoke give warming.
I smell them, I smell them, the bangers give no warning.

The stamping, the stamping, the gathered masses growing.
I hear them, I hear them, faster then all slowing.

It's brightening, it's brightening, the fire now is rising.
I see it, I see it, the flames that start enticing.

There's shrieking, there's shrieking, old and young are screaming.
I see them, I see them, the flaming barrels wheeling.

There's drinking, there's drinking, many revellers winking.
I smell them, I smell them, the fireworks high twinkling.

They're leaving, they're leaving, not much crowd remaining.
I hear them, I hear them, on the sea front fading.

It's ending, it's ending, bonfire now diminished.
We're sleepy, we're sleepy, as flames and fire finish…

``All happy, all happy, another year is passing.
Good people, good memories, of Hastings everlasting.

THE MODEL

I'm sure as I can be that Penny now is nude.
Disrobed, unclothed, slight veils here and there;
In nakedness, I find I am renewed.

I am not here with thoughts gone ripe and lewd,
But proudly showing Me I do declare:
I'm sure as I can be that Penny now is nude.

The curve and cut of me – you can't collude?
My frame, you say, is not the shape to bare.
In nakedness, I find I am renewed.

My corners and my creases are perused
By random hordes, the diffident who stare;
We're sure as we can be that Penny now is nude.

The scars I wear drag murmurs from this brood
With their fusty, brutal verdicts aired.
In nakedness, I find I am renewed.

Your prejudice, your views, hint turpitude –
I'll not accept the bias you declare.
I'm sure as I can be that Penny now is nude;
Such nakedness, I find I am renewed.

OH, BABY, YOU CAN

Oh, baby, you can
Stay up late and be damned

Oh, baby, you can
Play up bad and get banned

Oh, baby, you can
Wear those heels, with élan

Oh, baby, you can
Be with woman, be with man

Oh, honey, go free
Gulp on booze, do that weed

Oh, honey, you're free
To wallow in the sea

Oh, honey, be free
To climb your own tall tree

My lovely, it's fine
To dance and to dine

My lovely, it's fine
To love and to pine

My lovely, it's fine
To need to cry and whine

My lovely, it's fine
To not toe their line

Oh, baby, you can
Set your own life's plan

Oh, honey, you're free
To sometimes disagree

Oh, honey, you're free
In seeking liberty

My lovely, it's fine
To live your own design

A SONNET FOR BLUES AND RAIN

I heard the blues seduce the rain tonight
While owls sang songs to say that spring won't come.
They lurk in trees and whisper far from sight.
The blank sky shrugs down darkness. There among
The leaves I hid my heart and head and tears,
Drenched in the song the Blues Man gave to me,
Longing in my blood made sweeter with years.
Dark branches sway, they're full of melodies.
It's not love lost that aches inside my soul –
It's his true words that cry across the rain.
He sings the howling blues, he's in control,
Heals all my scars tonight, laps up my pain.
I will live for hidden owls, trees and hope,
The Blues Man's electric kaleidoscope.

ACKNOWLEDGEMENTS

In some ways this collection has taken a lifetime to complete, and there are many people I wish I could thank for those endless tiny moments that kept me going. Even if I can't name you all, I thank you all.

But the final gathering and honing of *Come Home Alive*, the tears and confidence drops were all gently moved along by outstanding support from a few individuals. John O'Donoghue, my friend, mentor and adopted big brother, holds my hand, kicks me nicely when he knows I can do better and reminds me how to play those words – always softly softly, Pen.

Extraordinary poet and critic – and super organiser – Dzifa Benson has worked with me for a year. Her insights and calm guidance have been invaluable in helping me to finalise the selection, and to feel comfortable with those choices. Gratitude also goes to all the great people at live literature organisation Renaissance One, who are responsible for the many new adventures in my life as a poet.

Many deep thanks must go to Theresa Hodge for her unstinting friendship and practical support, including loads of typing, and likewise to long-time bestie Steph S for serenely keeping me and my work in order.

Final thanks, of course, to the marvellous people at Burning Eye Books for their faith in my work – it's a privilege that my first collection is in your safe but, appropriately, not mainstream hands.